I0476507

# Money Makeover
## How to Manage Your Finances, Save Money, Get Out of Debt and Raise Your Credit Score

**Kash Carter**

Bella Vita Media

Carter, Kash

Money Makeover: How to Manage Your Finances, Save Money, Get Out of Debt and Raise Your Credit Score/Cash Carter.

# STOP!

Before you start reading, I've got a quick 7 second question for you...

How does getting all this awesomeness (for free) sound to you?

- A Free Excel Budget Template -
- Notifications of Upcoming Books -
- Occasional Budget Advice from the Author -

Pretty good, right?
Well, you can get it all by visiting the below link now.

## www.bellavitamedia.com

It's just a way for us to thank you for being a fan and supporter.

So, don't miss out. Check it out before you dive into your new book.

Thanks!

# Table of Contents

# Introduction

First and foremost, thank you and congratulations for purchasing this book and making the decision to take responsibility for your financial future.

Every day millions of Americans worry about how they will pay their rent next month, if the check they wrote yesterday will bounce today, and if they will be able to buy their kids new shoes, clothes and school supplies. They simply haven't learned ways to manage their money that will reduce these worries and put them on track to financial well-being.

This book will give you the foundation to begin planning for your financial future. It was written for the average person who lives paycheck to paycheck and doesn't see a way off the financial hamster wheel and out of debt. It is for those who don't believe they make enough to save, who feel that it's normal to struggle to make ends meet.

If that's not you, and you already have your finances in order, then you might already know most of the information presented in this book. But for those who are just beginning to think about their financial futures, those who want to start saving to make that big purchase or who are just thinking about college for their kids, please read on.

# Money

### What is Money?

Money is the current instrument of exchange or *mode* of exchange in the form of coins or bills. It is a way for an individual to trade what he possesses for what he desires.

## Myths about Money

There are various myths about money, for different people and cultures. Many people allow their beliefs about money control the way they spend, save and even the way they handle it.

When it comes to finances, many people believe they are doing as well as they possibly can. They may think they are accumulating savings, however they've never taken the time to sit down and figure out the math. They might be surprised if they did. Think about how these myths have influenced your spending in the past three months. Can you find any areas that need adjusting?

Here are some money saving myths many of people believe:

### *Savings accounts are the best way to save money*

Holding money for crises in a savings account is a great thought. But then again, if you want to save money, an out-of-date savings account may not be the best route to take. Unfortunately, with the state of today's economy, low interests rates don't keep up with increasing inflation.

Savings accounts are still a good idea if you want to save, but keep in mind, there are other methods to saving that yield higher interest, increasing your finances in the long run.

### Buying items on sale always saves money

Things may seem like they're a good price when they're on sat at 10%, 20% or even 30% off, but the reality is, you might not be saving any money. For some of us sale shopping is addicting, and instead of saving money, we spend unnecessarily. Often sale shopping results in spending twice as much as usual because we think we're saving and end up buying way too much. And, in the end we've overspent.

When shopping sales, it is better to buy what we really need and forego the things we simply want, especially when it's something that won't be used, worn or eaten.

*Tip: Combining coupons with sale prices, when possible, saves the most money. When done correctly can even get some items for free.

### Refinancing your home saves on interest

Refinancing your home doesn't necessarily mean you will save very much in the long run. It is true that the monthly payment is reduced, however it increases the amount of time you'll be paying for the home. Another 30-year term after having paid for the first 10 years mean you'll be paying for 40 years instead of the original 30. If you calculate the current payment and the previous payments, you might find you aren't actually saving anything.

If saving money on the mortgage is what you want, the best course is to refinance for a reduced rate and a shorter term. Your monthly payment may not decrease, but your total repayment could.

### 0% interest credit cards save money

When you obtain a credit card that has an initial interest rate of 0% for a specified amount of time, you'll save on interest in the beginning. However, when the interest rate kicks in, it is usually higher than you bargained for at 20% to 30%. If you fail to repay the total balance at the end of the interest free period, you'll end up paying for the items you purchased on the card, and the high interest rates. These cards are costlier than they appear.

When applying for credit cards, keep in mind that a high limit and a lower interest rate or a lower limit and a low interest rate are the best options. Interest free periods are bait and switch tactics.

### Savings depends on income

The amount of money you make does not make a difference or influence your saving capability. It is possible to save, even on a limited income. All you need to do is spend less than you earn, which is possible with budgeting. If you're spending money as soon as you make it, then it's impossible to save. As a matter of fact, you may possibly be spending a lot more than you bring in.

If you're waiting to make more money to begin saving, you may never start. Socking away even a dollar a day or a few dollars a week begins to add up.

*Tip: Use an empty pickle or mayonnaise jar to store change. When it fills up, roll the coins and deposit them in your savings. You might be surprised what you end up with at the end of the year.

# Your Money Blueprint

Our money blueprint guides our spending habits. It is our mindset about money; our deeply held beliefs about the way money should be treated. Our money blueprint was instilled in us during childhood, and comes from our parents' beliefs about money. As a result we are conditioned to behave either negatively or positively with money. If we grew up in a frugal household we be more frugal. If we grew up in a wasteful household we might be more likely to spend frivolously.

"Money doesn't grow on trees."

"Don't spend money you don't have."

"Money can't buy happiness."

These are phrases many of us heard growing up, and whether we know it or not, they have affected our feelings about money into adulthood. Because of this many of us are already pre-programmed either struggle or prosper financially. If we grew up in a frugal household we may be more frugal.

Although our money blueprint is deeply entrenched in our subconscious, it is possible to change our money mindset.

To rid ourselves of money issues and get on the right financial track once and for all, we have to reset our thinking.

## Find Out Your Money Blueprint

Here is a brief and basic technique to help figure out your financial blueprint.

Take out a pencil and a sheet of paper. Start by asking yourself fundamental questions regarding money. Get a pencil and paper and jot down all of your feelings, thoughts and experiences as they pertain to money. Write down everything, even if they seem silly, embarrassing or weird.

Ask yourself:

1.  What are my beliefs about money?

    Write down everything that comes to mind. Continue asking yourself this question until you've run out of answers. When you're done, move on to the next question.

2.  What are my parents' beliefs about money? (Ask your parents.)

    Write down everything that comes to mind. Continue asking yourself this question until you've run out of answers. When you're done, move on to the next question.

3.  Who am I similar to when it comes to money? (Your money blueprint is probably similar to your parents. Were they savers or spenders? Were they avoiders? Did they manage money well or did they often mismanage? Were they investors? Did they educate you on how to deal with money? Are you repeating their money practices? )

    Write down everything that comes to mind. Continue asking yourself this question until you've run out of answers. When you're done, move on to the next question

4.  What are my spending and saving habits?

    Write down everything that comes to mind. Continue asking yourself this question until you've run out of answers. When you're done, move on to the next question.

5.  Did any events happen that molded my beliefs regarding

money?
Examples: eviction, running out of food, receiving a
windfall like inheritance or winnings.

Write down everything that comes to mind. Continue
asking yourself this question until you've run out of
answers. When you're done, move on to the next question.

6.  Am I content to make just enough to get by, or is my goal
    to make hundreds, thousands, hundreds of thousands or
    millions of dollars?

    Write down everything that comes to mind. Continue
    asking yourself this question until you've run out of
    answers. When you're done, move on to the next question.

7.  What are your values and priorities?

    Place the following values in order of significance to you:
    Love, Health, Safety, Security, Honesty, Comfort, Money,
    Education, Integrity.

If money doesn't fall in your top three, it probably isn't a
priority in your life. More than likely, you don't put enough
time and energy into managing it.

When you've answered all of the questions go over your list.
Combine two to three related answers into one, if possible.
Next determine whether you feel each answer is negative or
positive. Finally put a plus sign (+) after every answer you
believe is an advantage toward achieving your financial goals,
and a negative sign (-) after every point you believe is a
disadvantage toward achieving your financial goals.

This record will be your MONEY BLUEPRINT on paper. All
the negative points, are those that restrict your capability of
obtaining financial freedom. The more negatives there are, the

more limited are your abilities of becoming financially stable.

If you have more negatives than positives then you have to re-adjust your money blueprint. Until you do, you will continue to have difficulties with money. In order to do this, you have to change how you think about money.

It's a fact that rich people think differently about money and treat money differently than people who have little money. Another way to change our money blueprint is to begin to think the way they do.

Here are few ways rich people think act behave:

1. Rich people don't overspend; they live below their means. If a purchase will put them farther from their financial goals, they forego the purchase. They don't take out loans and go into debt to buy something they want. Instead, they think about money so they can make more to raise their means and make those extravagant purchases.

   If you want to buy that car, that house, high-priced item, consider how it will affect your financial goals. If it's going to set you back instead of build you up, put it off, make more money then buy it when you can afford it.

2. Rich people think long-term. They plan for their financial futures and make decisions accordingly. When they make financial decisions they consider whether it will be beneficial or detrimental to their financial goals. They delay gratification in order to be wealthier tomorrow.

   Again, if that expensive purchase is going to put a dent in your wallet or bank account, or increase your credit card debt, leave it alone until your account is healthy enough to withstand the blow.

3. Rich people teach their children to be rich and to know the

value of a dollar. They prepare their children to handle a large amounts so that they understand that mishandling money can lead to it all being squandered away.

Early financial education is the best way to ensure your children don't develop an unhealthy relationship with money and spending. Children should learn to be rich, even if they don't come from a rich family.

4. Rich people take risks. They know that failure is always possible but they don't let it keep them from making the decisions that may make them successful. If failure happens they pick themselves up and continue moving forward.

    Fear of failure results in inaction. It's okay to take financial risks when the possibility of success is greater than the possibility of failure. Even if you fail, you can pick yourself up and keep going.

5. Rich people surround themselves with likeminded people. Successful people befriend other successful people. The same can be said for most people in almost every tax bracket.

    If you want to elevate yourself financially, it's best to find other people who aspire to the same level of financial success. People who plan for success do better when they are around other people who plan for success.

# Create a Personal Financial Blueprint

A financial blueprint serves as a plan for your financial growth and stability. Much like the blueprint for a house, this is the vision for the way your finances will look after a given period of time.

The blueprint is the framework of the larger plan. Spending, investing and saving all fall into this framework. The financial blueprint should be the first thing you consider and the basis for all major financial decisions.

The first step to creating a financial blueprint is to **establish clearly defined financial goals**. When we have defined and written out our goals, they become tangible. We can see them and take actionable steps to achieve them.

Example:

My goal is to save $2000 over the next twelve months.

Steps: Save $77.00 from each paycheck in a high interest savings account, until I've reached my goal.

On a bi-weekly pay schedule, with 26 pay periods in a year, I'd save $2002 over twelve months, not including the accumulated interest.

The next step to creating a financial blueprint is to **develop a budget**. A budget makes it easier to plot out just how much you will spend, save and/or invest. We will discuss how to create a budget in detail in the next chapter.

For many people retirement is a major concern. You can develop your financial blueprint to include retirement planning.

Your financial blueprint may also include college funds if you or your children plan to attend college and you want to mitigate student loan debt.

Investment plans, stocks and other savings methods can all go into the financial blueprint.

The financial blueprint is your personal plan to obtain financial freedom and is yours to create the way you wish.

Financial planners are there to help you work out your financial blueprint, however they come at a cost. If you are comfortable paying for advice on creating a financial plan then you might want to search out a planner in your price range, who will listen to your goals and consider your circumstances, and take your financial future seriously.

If a financial planner isn't for you, there are several FREE apps, and online tools to help build your financial blueprint. At the very least, they can help you get started on a budget and keep track of spending.

# Create a Budget

We all know we should create a budget, but many of us either just don't want to make one or don't know where to start.

A *budget* is the best way to plan for and keep track of your monthly income and expenses. It will help to determine how much is coming in, how much is going out and how much is left over. It will also help to determine if what's left should be saved or can be spent on wants rather than needs. Budgets also come in handy when it comes to debt management.

In order to gain control over debt, it is important to set up a budget and maintain it. This is the tricky part. It takes a certain level of commitment on the part of the individual to stick to the budget. Otherwise, it just becomes a plan that is never implemented.

That is where most people fail. They do manage to set up a budget, but after a few weeks, for whatever reason, they stray from what the plan.

### How to Set Up a Budget

Budgeting doesn't have to be painful or difficult. One of the reasons people avoid budgeting like the plague is because it means making tough decisions about "cutting back" or "making sacrifices".

Here are a few actionable steps to take in order to create a budget:

Step 1: Know how much you have.

> If you have savings, or investments, check your account balances and write them down. Checking account balances too, write them down.

Step 2: Know where your money comes from.

Identify all your sources of incomes i.e. job, child support, disability or unemployment, etc.

To make your budget more realistic, only use fixed earnings, or those that you are sure to receive. Uncertain income such as tips, a potential raise, or a commission-based bonus should be excluded.

Step 3: Know where your money goes.

Identify your expenses. It helps to use categories.

- Fixed expenses like rent or mortgage, car payment, childcare, insurance, etc.

- Basic necessities, i.e. groceries, clothing, gas, etc.

- Discretionary expenses i.e. gifts, dining out, entertainment, etc.

To figure out how much you spend, save all your receipts for a 30-day period and refer to them when calculating average monthly expenses. It also helps to go over previous month's bank statements and check your transaction history. Get receipts from gas station purchases, especially if you use cash.

There are also several different tools and software products that you can use to keep track of your actual income and expenses. There are several free apps and online tools to help develop a budget if you are not comfortable doing it the old-school way of using pen and paper.

Step 3: Know how much you owe.

You should already have an idea how much you are

paying for your various debts every month. However, you should also find out the total amount of debt you currently have, and this encompasses your various loans, mortgages, and even credit cards.

Step 4: Compare your income and expenses.

By examining your income versus your expenses, you will immediately know whether you are overspending, spending just right, or spending so little you have extra money each month. This will then guide you on where your budgeting will go next.

If your expenses exceed your income you need to examine where you need to reduce spending.

- Make cuts. When you logged your expenses, you categorized them according to the nature of the expense. You may also use the log to refine the list further, classifying them according to necessity. Identify the expenses that are not necessary and cut them out.

- Make adjustments. Some experts recommend categorizing expenses in two ways: needs and wants (and the identification should be done objectively). When making a trip to the grocery store, list the items you need and set a spending limit for only those items. Purchase items on the want list only if there is enough money left after all other expenses are taken care of.

- Look for alternatives to spending. For example, instead of going to the movies four times in a month, you may want to cut it down to only twice a month. Ask yourself: Do I really need to pay to watch the IMAX version when the regular theater is $3.00 less? And why buy movie theater candy when the local discount store has the same thing for $0.99?

Step 5: Treat "Savings" as a regular expense.

Decide on an amount to regularly put into your savings account, or any other savings vehicle, such as stock investments and financial instruments. If you can set aside 10% of your take-home pay every month and do this on a recurring basis, as you would an expense, you'll increase your savings faster. If your job offers direct deposit, you can have a portion of your check deposited into savings every pay period. That way you don't have to think about it.

Step 6: Test your budget.

Don't expect the first few weeks of putting your budget into action to be easy. There will be a transition period as you change your spending habits. sHowever, do not make that an excuse not to follow the budget diligently.

Keep detailed records of your daily spending for at least a month; this will help you assess whether your budget is working, and if you are truly adhering to the plan.

You should also use the testing period as an opportunity to make necessary adjustments. It is possible that you overlooked some expenses or other factors while you were drafting your budget.

**Tips for an Effective Budget**

A budget is never set in stone. There will be constant adjustments as circumstances change. Priorities change, and unavoidable situations demand that changes be made.

In order to ensure the budget remains effective, however, here are some simple tips that could help.

> Keep it simple. Many people don't stick with their budget because they're too overwhelmed by the smallest details. Keep things simple if detail orientation isn't your strong suit. If you personally prepared the budget, however, this shouldn't be a problem.

> Keep it realistic. Budgeting makes use of estimates, but these estimates are based on actual, historical figures. Don't pull amounts or numbers out of thin air or without basis. Otherwise, you're just setting your budget – and yourself – up for failure.

> Value substance over form. So what if your recordkeeping is less than systematic? It doesn't matter if your budget is written in a small notebook instead or a spreadsheet. As long as you understand what you've written, and it contains all the necessary information, you are doing great.

> Stick to it. The most difficult part of a budget is sticking to it. Just remind yourself why you're doing this and what the end result will be.

# Eliminate Debt

## (Knowing When You Have a Debt Problem)

Overall well-being does not only refer to physical, mental and emotional health. Financial wellness contributes to our well-being as well. Unfortunately, some of us overlook, or worse, deliberately ignore our financial health when it comes to debt.

But, there are times when we have to take some time out and take stock of our finances, and not just how much we earn and spend. It is easy ignore the amount of debt we've incurred until we apply for a loan, want to rent a house or even get a job. That's when our credit scores reveal just how much debt we truly have.

One indicator of financial health is one's debt-to-income ratio. Experts recommend that a person owe, at most, 20% of their net take-home pay. For example, a person earning $1000 a month should keep his debt below $200 a month. If his car payment is that amount, he shouldn't think about incurring other debts.

But that is an ideal situation, and the reality is that most of us owe far more than 20% of our monthly pay. We still tend to find ourselves buried up to our eyeballs in debt, and often feel helpless as to how to get out of it.

**Common Causes of Debt Problems**

Debt problems, or "credit problems" can be caused by several behaviors. The most common causes are listed below:

1. Overspending, or spending beyond one's financial means

2. Reckless spending, or incurring unnecessary expenses

3. Poor budgeting, which can be either the inability to come up with a budget, or failure to adhere to a budget which is already in place

4. Making bad investments

5. Unforeseen circumstances, such as emergencies, job loss, health issues, and even death

So how do you know when you have a debt problem? If you've ever found yourself in any of the following situations, you may have debt and credit problems.

- You are often late in paying, or scrambling to meet your payment due dates.

- You tap into your savings to pay bills and even basic necessities such as groceries.

- More than half of your monthly income goes towards paying debts.

- You are no longer able to add to your savings.

- You have no savings, period.

- You use credit cards, or borrow money from other people, to pay for regular items that you used to pay for using cash, such as groceries, medicines, and even meals.

- You are use cash advances from your credit cards to pay off other bills.

- You can pay only the minimum payments on your credit cards.

- You've maxed more than one credit card.

- Your credit card balances increase every month due to continuous purchases, despite you making regular payments.

- You no know exactly how much you owe.

- You constantly argue with family members about money.

- You avoid calls from creditors and collectors.

- You're several months behind on bill payments.

- Your bank account is overdrawn or you've bounced a check or two.

- You have experienced being denied credit.

You may have experienced another example that wasn't listed, but they are all serious and must be remedied.

If you lost your job tomorrow would you be able to get by – paying for your basic necessities AND paying your debts – until you find another job?

If someone in your family suddenly fell ill and you had to shoulder all the medical bills, would you be able to survive financially?

If you are more than sure that you'd face immediate financial crisis if one of the above happened, then it is safe to say that you have a debt problem. It's time to take action to prevent it from turning into a major disaster.

# Repay Debts and Raise Your Credit Score

Your financial blueprint will be an integral part of your debt repayment strategy. Furthermore, there are a number of actions you should take when planning to repay debts.

- Stick to repayment schedules.

  Loans have respective repayment schedules that you must stick to. Otherwise, you end up paying more, due to late fees, penalties, and other charges.

  Credit card loans have payment due dates specified the billing statements. Depending on the credit card issuer, there is usually a grace period for paying before the due date where the purchase doesn't incur a finance charge. You do not want to have to pay late fees and exorbitant interest rates due to failure to pay on time.

- Prioritize the debts to be paid.

  As much as you want to pay off all your debts all at once, your financial circumstances may not allow it. Therefore, you'll need to prioritize which debts have to be paid first. In order to do that, you must make a list of all your debts, with the relevant information indicated, such as the interest rates, repayment period, balances, and minimum monthly payments, if any.

  Here are some options you could look into:

  ➤ Prioritize debts according to simple interest rates.

    In this strategy, you'll pay off the debts with highest interest rates first. You may want to talk to your lender or credit card company to find out if you can have the rate lowered beforehand. This will decrease your monthly minimum, enable you to pay them off faster, and help you save money, as well.

Many credit card companies are willing to lower interests rates to retain customers. It never hurts to ask.

➢ Prioritize debts according to effective interest rates.

Unlike simple interest, effective interest rates take into account the tax effect. This is seen more frequently in student loans, mortgages, and similar loan types.

Prioritize debts according to other fees.

There are some loans or debts that have other fees apart from interest. If the fees are substantial, it could affect your decision on which debt to pay first. There are a few ways to handle these.

• Avoid the "minimum payment syndrome".

Credit card bills give you a minimum payment to keep the account current. Many credit card owners simply pay that amount not realizing the minimum basically only covers the interest. Throwing in an extra $5 can help decrease the principal amount faster.

• Apply the "Snowball" or "Snowflaking" technique.

This is a repayment option applicable to credit card debts (and it's the only instance where paying the minimum monthly payment is actually encouraged). If you have several credit cards, rank them according to their interest rates.

Pay off as much as you can on the first debt – the one with the highest interest rate. Pay the minimum monthly payments on the other credit cards.

Once the first debt has been paid off, move on to the one with the second highest interest rate, paying as much as you can and paying only the minimum monthly payments on the others.

- Negotiate with lenders.

There is nothing wrong with talking to your lenders. Debtors are advised to always be honest with lenders. Relationships that involve lending or borrowing money require a certain level of trust, which is why it is important to be straightforward with them.

Negotiating with lenders can result in better terms. Again, you can ask them to lower your interest rate, which may decrease your minimum payment and make it easier to pay down the principal. You could also ask them lengthen the loan term or period which gives you more time to pay off the debt.

## How to Avoid the Negative Impact of Interest

You must be wondering why the debt payment prioritization puts a lot of weight on interest, the amount (which is usually a certain percentage of the amount of principal) to be paid by the debtor to the creditor on top of the principal. It is the fee charged by the lender to a borrower for the use of borrowed money.

Essentially, the concept of interest states that it takes more money to borrow money.

Usually, the interest is calculated into monthly payment, as is the case with car payments and home loans. The interest on credit cards is also factored into the minimum payment.

Interest rates have a negative impact on debt once they begin to increase. As you repay debt, interest rates can pose bigger problems.

For example, the case of credit card debts. As mentioned earlier, a greater chunk of the minimum payments covers the interest more than the original debt. When you are trying to pay off a debt with high interest rates, you will also be paying more toward the finance charge instead of the principal, which means it will take you longer pay off that debt.

The only thing you can do to avoid this is to pay more than the minimum payments specified. Increase your monthly payment so you will be able to pay more of the outstanding principal, which is used as the basis of computing the interest. Naturally, as the amount of outstanding loan decreases, the amount of interest you will pay will also decrease, even if the interest rate remains constant.

## Avoid Further Debt

Once you've gotten yourself out of debt, you will probably feel like a weight has been lifted off your shoulders. But it doesn't stop there.

At this stage, you should adopt a "been there, done that, and never again" attitude. You have already experienced what it is like to be saddled with debts, and you have done everything possible in order to be rid of them. Once you've succeeded, it's time to ensure that it never happens again.
Here are very simple tips on how you can continue to have full control over your debt status or, simply, to be free from debt.

1. Use credit cards sparingly.

   "Retail therapy" is a very common practice among people who feel down and want to cheer themselves up. The buying process releases dopamine into their systems, which makes them feel happy. It's another reason for shopping addiction.

If shopping is your habit and you are a compulsive spender, use cash instead of credit. If you absolutely must use a credit card, pay off the balance during the grace period, BEFORE interest is attached to the balance, which is usually 28 days after the purchase (check with your credit card company).

Shop only when you truly need to buy something. Do not be easily swayed by ads, brochures and catalogs. If you're the type to buy items and never use them, not only will you save money, you'll also save space in your home.

2. Set some money aside for emergencies.

Experts recommend that everyone have at least six months of living expenses saved up. If you should lose your job today, you'd need to know exactly how you'd keep a roof over your head, food on your table and clothes on yours and your family's backs.

An emergency fund will help keep you from relying on credit cards should you lose your job, your car breaks down or you end up with a huge medical bill.

3. Avoid applying for loans

After paying off a debt, the last thing you want to do is enter into another one. If you must buy something that costs so much that you need to take out a loan, you should consider if it's something you really need. You should consult your financial blueprint, and decide if that loan is worth derailing your financial progress.

4. Look for other sources of additional income.

Bringing in extra money can mitigate debt

exponentially. If you have the time or need to supplement your income part-time jobs, garage sales, and small side businesses are a few of the options you could look into. We will discuss potential sources of extra income in a later chapter.

5. Set up a financial documents file.

Receipts, bills, bank statements… anything that has to do with your money, file them accordingly. Keep a log, ledger or file folder of your debts, and update them with payments and other transactions affecting them, complete with the date you made the transaction.

Not only is it prudent recordkeeping; it's also a way to protect yourself should your lenders come after you for a payment you've already made. You will have documentation to back up your dispute (e.g. receipts, bills). You can create your own record keeping system for this.

6. Get help.

There's no shame in seeking help from a professional to learn to manage your credit and your finances.

Approaching a credit counselor for advice can be the best option for a given situation. There are plenty experts who provide credit counseling services to people in serious financial distress. They assess your financial situation and offer reasonable solutions.

Another advantage of using to a credit counselor is their ability to help create a debt management plan. They can find ways to make your debts more manageable, so you can be free of them sooner than you thought.

# Obtain Credit Reports

Your credit score is the way that most lenders determine whether or not they want to risk loaning you money. It is a measure of your debt-to-income ratio and the way creditors grade your payment history with lenders. Unfortunately too many of us don't know our credit scores and are surprised when we learn that they are not as high as we thought.

In order to raise your credit score, you first have to know who and what you owe. And, the best way to find out and keep an eye on your debt is obtain your credit reports from each of the three credit reporting bureaus. Once a year, consumers are allowed a free report from each of these companies: TransUnion, Equifax and Experian.

Creditors report to at least one of these companies. The bureaus keep track of how much you each creditor, if your account is current, and how many days delinquent your account is. This is a great way to find out exactly who you owe if you can't remember all the loans and accounts you have opened.

By monitoring your reports you can also catch any inaccuracies that might bring down your credit score. If you find any false or outdated information, you can dispute it to have it removed from your report. 25% of people find incorrect information on their reports.

Another method to monitor your score is to sign up with a credit monitoring service. Credit Karma is a free service that provides your TransUnion and Equifax scores as well as notifies you when a change has been made to your credit report.

Repaying debts is the first way to improve your credit score. The next way is to establish a good payment history. When you begin paying off your debts, you establish a payment history that each creditor reports to the bureaus. The better your repayment history, the more your score improves. Since you can only receive each report once a year, you might want to stagger your requests. This way you'll be able to monitor one report every four months.

Example:

In January you request your report from Experian. Then, you request your report from Equifax in May. Finally you request your report from Transunion in September. This keeps your reports revolving so you can monitor any new activity and dispute any new negative information.

# Tackle Student Loans

Because of their high balances, student loan debt can be the most damaging to your credit score. Handling student loan debt requires time and patience. Aside from the fact monthly payments can be exorbitantly high, especially if you're an unemployed recent graduate. There are, however, ways to delay payments, reduce payments, and even have the loans forgiven. These options are specific to federal student loans. Private loan companies may have different requirements and payment options.

You require a proactive attitude when dealing with student loan debts particularly when you have additional disbursements to make for instance car loan or credit card bills. Studying associated loans commonly have a reduced interest rate as contrasted to credit card debt. This insinuates that you ought to give attention to first settling down your credit card dues before your student loan dues. On the other hand you are certainly lucky if you simply possess a student loan arrears.

Certain studying related loans permits you to do payment for an interlude of ten years by way of a monthly payment arrangement. All the same, you even so ought to have plans to save money. Here are a couple of pointers to efficiently drop your costs.

### Graduated Payments

Before trying to take on the task of tackling student loans, you'll need to contact your lenders. They will try to work with you to come up with a feasible payment arrangement. If the arrangement becomes too difficult you can have your due date changed or even as have the plan changed.

## Income Contingent Repayment

Some lenders offer an income-driven payment arrangement, where your payment is based on your monthly income. Speak to your loan servicer to determine your eligibility.

## Loan Consolidation

Loan consolidation is another effective approach to handling student loans. If you have multiple student loans with different interest rates, then consolidating all your loans into one will enable you to pay them off altogether at a fixed interest rate. You can also lower the aggregate payment and also be able to spread your repayment time. An additional advantage you can gain because of loan consolidation is that you are able to enhance your credit.

## Deferment and Forbearance

As your loan repayment grace period approaches you may need to delay payments due to unemployment, temporary disability or other personal reasons. Federal student loans servicers can give you a decrement or forbearance. Both options allow you to postpone payments for a designated period of time. Your lender will determine which you qualify for.

It is important to note that although payments are postponed during deferment and forbearance, the loan still accrues interest during that time, which means your loan will have increased by the end of your deferment or forbearance period.

## Loan Forgiveness

Depending on your specific circumstances, your student loan may be discharged altogether. Certain loans may be forgiven and people in certain industries may be eligible to have their loans cancelled or discharged. For information on qualifying you should visit the Federal Student Aid website,

Total permanent disability discharge allows for people who are disabled and unable to obtain employment to have certain loans discharged with proof of disability.

Regardless of the course you choose to take, student loan debts have to be taken care of. Your credit report will take a major hit when your student loans default from repeated non-repayment. To keep your score at a healthy number, it's advisable to work with your student loan lenders to find the best option for repayment.

# Develop Money Management Skills

Developing a budget and sticking to it is a great start to money management. However, there are other money management skills and strategies – most of them practical – that you can develop and apply in order have greater control over your money and become debt-free.

Money management skills are not something you are born with. They are learned and developed over time.

- Set new up accounts (if needed).

  It would be a good idea to open accounts in order to improve money management.

  One account that you must open is a savings account. Savings is a part of your budget and your financial blueprint, so if you don't have a savings account now is the time to get one. If you've committed to saving a certain percentage of your monthly income it should be deposited into a savings account. Open a regular deposit account for savings at your bank where that amount will be deposited.

  Again, if your employer offers direct deposit, you can have a specified amount deposited into your savings account. Another way to make it easy is to schedule an automatic transfer from your checking to your savings. This can even be done between banks if your savings happens to be a different bank than your checking.

  If you are more forward-thinking, you might also open a specialized retirement account. Those who have second jobs or another source of additional income can funnel even half of their added income to this account.

Once you have set up these accounts, make sure not to make any withdrawals UNLESS ABSOLUTELY NECESSARY. The longer you keep them in the bank, the more interest they will earn.

- Learn to balance your checkbook.

  Monthly reconciliation and balancing of your checkbook is highly recommended since it is a way to track movement of money.

- Maintain good relationships with creditors and lenders.

  You will have an easier time managing your money and your debt if you have a good relationship with your creditors and lenders. You will also have greater chances of being granted concessions if you get into a bind when the bill is due.

- Set up a "due date calendar".

  When you keep track of due dates it is easier to avoid late fees. Setting up a calendar will also give you more than enough time to plan your payments and reconfigure your spending plan, if necessary.

# Save Money Daily

There are ways to save money in every aspect of our daily lives. With the financial state of the United States and Europe, it seems everyone could find new ways to cut spending and save money. If you depend on paycheck to paycheck as majority us of do, then you had better, no, you have to buckle down right away so you ensure something allocated for retirement. Minor changes to everyday living can bring about a huge influence throughout the years to come.

1. **Couponing**

   Couponing can result in massive savings per shopping trip. Each and every time you set out to the grocery store, here are means by which you are be able to save money.

   The Sunday paper is a great place to find coupons for food and household items. At the beginning of every month, the Sunday paper distributes the Brand Saver coupon book, which offers more than $100 in savings on products from razors to toilet paper.

   Budget and preplan your trip. Make a grocery list before leaving the house.

   Purchase items you use on a regular basis in bulk or in greater amounts always cheaper.

   Check couponing websites to match coupons with current and upcoming sales and deals.

   If you need something and don't have a coupon, go for generic products as a replacement for brand name.

   Check expiration dates on products while at the grocery store and purchase products with the furthest date from the date of purchase. Use reusable grocery bags. Many stores offer $0.05 per bag used instead of paper or plastic, and in some cities, using plastic will cost $0.05 per bag and up.

Once you get home and put your groceries away, ensure to store the bags if you're not using reusable bags. Plastic bags happen to be perfect trash bags for small cans, on the other hand paper bags are versatile for carrying items as well as for craft projects and textbook covers. This way you are saving a lot of money by utilizing free products.

2. **Debt and Bills**

The faster you pay off your credit cards, the more you save in the long run. You might not be able to pay them off immediately, but the more you can pay, the less interest you'll incur. Putting off payments incurs late fees and more interest, and paying consistently improves your payment history and credit score.

You might find it helpful to set up recurring payments from your bank account through online banking. That way you don't have to worry about making payments on time, they're taken care of for you. However, if you do use this option, you'll have to watch your account closely and make sure to overdraw.

3. **Entertainment**

Movies and concerts add up, especially when saving is the goal. The cost of tickets and refreshments just compound the price. The better option would be to hit the DVD rental kiosk and the local grocery store to rent a movie for $1.67/night and stock up on popcorn, candy and drinks.

Sure, you might not being seeing the latest movie on the big screen (unless you have a big screen TV), but you're saving an average of $8.17 per ticket, $8.15 for large popcorn, $6.31 for a large drink and $4.25 for a large candy. That's a savings of 26.88 per person.

If you have to go the movies, try to hit a matinee, which costs less than an evening show.

4. **Dining Out**

Dining out is nice, but one meal at a nice restaurant can easily cost more than a tank of gas. Which, at this point may be upward of $60.00 for a 15-gallon tank. To save money, opt for a new cookbook and some fresh ingredients. Improving your culinary skills can be fun, and there are plenty of recipe websites that can turn your regular meatloaf dinner into Gourmet burgers.

If you have a habit of getting lunch from the food truck or hitting the fast food restaurant on the corner every day, you'll benefit from brown bagging it even a few days a week. Not only will you keep money in your pockets, you might drop a few needed pounds as well.

5. **Bargain Hunting**

With a little research, it's easy to find products at a reduced price. One of the best places to find good items at major discounts is online. Even brand new, high-end, genuine designer items, are sold on eBay and other websites at a fraction of their retail price. Not only are you able to purchase items on eBay, you can also effortlessly establish a sellers account to trade your personal items and make money. Buying online will save you on quite much everything.

You can as well find discounts in classified ads. Every weekend people hold garage sales and it is very easy to find things you might be looking for from furniture to children's items to housewares to electronics. Estate sales usually offer the most items and it's easy to haggle with previous owners to get rock bottom prices.

Secondhand and thrift stores. The Salvation Army and the Goodwill are just two of the many stores that offer the lowest prices on items you may be in search of.

6.  **Saving Around The House**

    There are numerous methods you can exercise to save money in your home. Get the entire family on board and save.

    - Turn off lights in rooms that aren't in use.

    - Turn down the thermostat a few degrees.

    - Use energy saving light bulbs.

    - Use a power strip for electronics and turn it off when leaving the house.

    - Hang your clothes to dry (if possible.)

    - Buy energy efficient appliances.

    - Have windows and doors sealed to prevent heat loss.

    *Tip: Electric companies have programs to help homes improve energy efficiency, so check with them about sealing doors and windows. They might do it for free if your income qualifies. Let all family members know that you've begun a savings plan so they can get involved. They might be able to help find further savings.

    - Quit smoking. Giving up a pack-a-day or more habit can easily put extra cash back into your pockets. Not to mention the health benefits.

    *Tip: If you manage to quit, put the money you would have spent on cigarettes for the day or week in a jar, or better yet, into your savings account. It will quickly increase your savings.

In the beginning you man not see enormous savings, but at the end of the month, when you go over your budget you might notice a significant difference. At the end of the year, if you've stuck to your financial blueprint you might find you've saved hundreds of dollars on every day expenses.

# Make More Money

The cold hard truth is that in order to build wealth, saving just isn't enough. We have to make more money. Money problems don't simply come from too much spending, although it's a major contributor. The fact is, not having enough income is what causes problems for many of us. For this reason, we should consider our income sources and make the conscious decision to make more.

**Unique and Creative Ways to Make Money**

Sure, making more money sounds easier said than done, but there are several methods to bring in extra cash. Finding a higher paying job, with the job market as it is, probably isn't realistic, but thinking outside of the box might just lead you to creating your own side business.

Some of these methods can earn you a second income, which may help supplement your income and reach your financial goals sooner. Others good for making a little extra spending cash for incidentals like a tank of gas. Either way, with a little creativity and determination, you can put extra money in your pockets or your bank account.

*Make Money Selling Online*

As mentioned earlier, the internet offers a plethora of opportunities. If your one those who have things around the house that are no longer in use, you can cash in using eBay. If your items are in good condition, and they're taking up valuable space in your home, why not turn them into profit?

If you have a creative side and are good at crafting eBay isn't the only option. There are several websites that allow you to list your creations for the price you set. The fees are extremely reasonable and you can list as many items as you'd like. Many people have parlayed these websites into home businesses that cover many of their household expenses.

Affiliate marketing is another option for selling online. In this case, you sell products via an affiliate link located on your own website. You receive a commission each time someone makes a purchase through your affiliate link. You have to have your own website account for this option. Obtaining a website is simple. Several web hosts now offer free websites. All you have to do is choose a host, set up your account, and build your site.

### Online Data Entry Jobs

Several companies nowadays outsource data entry jobs to online freelancers to reduce costs. By hiring individuals to work from home, businesses are able to cut down their expenses and increase profits.

There a several freelance websites where people offer their services and set their own hourly rate. When a job is available they bid on it and, if awarded, get paid for a few hours work from home. If you have a full-time or part-time job, working from home might be a great way to supplement your income.

### Become a Mystery Shopper

If you enjoy shopping, becoming a mystery shopper might be right up your alley. Companies pay regular people to visit stores, restaurants, and auto shops to rate and review their shopping experiences. An online search of reputable mystery companies will turn up a plethora of mystery shopping companies that are looking for people for daily shopping.

Although mystery shopping won't pay as much as freelance work, it's a great way to get out of the house. Many jobs that require a purchase will reimburse the cost of the items and also pay a bonus for shopping experience.

### Online Surveys

Like secret shopping, companies are willing to pay you for your feedback via surveys. You provide your opinion on products and services you already use by answering questions via online survey forms. Surveys are free and take as little as five to ten minutes to complete.

These are just a few ways to make extra money. With a little time and research you can find plenty of other ways to make extra in your spare time.

# Conclusion

For some, being debt-free can seem like a pipe dream. However, everyone can be debt free with careful planning, diligent money management, and goal setting.

Everyone has the right to financial freedom and security. By developing a healthy relationship with money by developing your financial blueprint and protecting your finances by limiting debt you are well on you way to a bright future, for you and your family.

The road to becoming debt free may seem like a long and bumpy one, but the skills you've learned in this book, it should be easier than you thought. It may take baby steps at first, but keep in mind that every journey starts with a single step.

You have already taken the first step by reading this book and making the conscious decision to take control of your finances!

Finally, if you enjoyed this book, then I'd like to ask you for a favor, would you be kind enough to leave a review for this book on Amazon? It'd be greatly appreciated.

Thank you and good luck!

# STOP!

Before you start reading, I've got a quick 7 second question for you...

How does getting all this awesomeness (for free) sound to you?

- A Free Excel Budget Template -
- Notifications of Upcoming Books -
- Occasional Budget Advice from the Author -

Pretty good, right?
Well, you can get it all by visiting the below link now.

www.bellavitamedia.com

It's just a way for us to thank you for being a fan and supporter.

So, don't miss out. Check it out before you dive into your new book.

Thanks!

www.ingramcontent.com/pod-product-compliance
Lightning Source LLC
Chambersburg PA
CBHW070922180526
45168CB00005B/2115